1001

Your Key to Successful Events!

AWESOME

Conference, Meeting & Event

THEMES

A helpful resource for event planners, leaders, coaches, authors & ministers

Interior & cover layout & design:
Tarsha L. Campbell

Published by:

DOMINIONHOUSE
Publishing & Design, LLC
P.O. Box 681938
Orlando, Florida 32868
www.mydominionhouse.com
407.703.4800

DEDICATION

This book is dedicated to every person who plans conferences, meetings or special events or desires to do so. May you realize the privilege you have been given to plan gatherings that bring ideas and people together, ultimately changing the course of lives, corporations and organizations. It is my wish that this book will empower you tremendously by getting you started with an awesome theme!

"Unity is powerful! There's nothing like bringing people together under a corporate anointing in a conference or special event to unify them under God's purpose and agenda. The environment is set for divine acceleration and advancement."

-- T.L. Campbell --

ACKNOWLEDGMENTS

To my husband, Dwayne. Thank you for always believing in me and allowing me to walk out my purpose and step into my destiny. You will always be my hero. You're one of God's greatest gifts to me.

To my mom, Pastor Betty Jamison. Thank you for always giving me the freedom to plan life-changing events and conferences for your organization over the years. It's through this freedom I tapped into one of the many gifts the Father has placed in me.

"Putting together great content

for a conference and special

event starts with clarifying your

purpose and objectives,

and choosing

an awesome theme."

-- T.L. Campbell --

TABLE OF CONTENTS

Section I:

Keys Needed to Plan Your Awesome Event

Section II:

Theme Categories

TABLE OF CONTENTS

TABLE OF CONTENTS

Chapter 1:

What's a Theme and

Why Do I Need One?

I love conferences! I'm not what some call a "conference junkie," hopping from conference to conference trying to get some type of emotional or spiritual fix. I do, however, value every conference and special event I have strategically attended that has informed, empowered and catapulted me to a new level of understanding and well-being, plus given me that extra boost to keep moving forward.

It's from these special events I have come to realize the power of corporate gatherings to unify a cause, restore relationships, bring healing, build community and empower individuals for the betterment of society at large.

One common thread that I have noticed flowing through each of these special events has been a theme.

A theme, in and of itself, is what sets the stage for each conference, meeting and special event. A theme is the centralized focus of the event. It establishes the tone for what will be covered and discussed throughout your gathering and sessions.

A theme will substantiate what your goals are for the event and make sure everyone involved, from speakers to those who volunteer, are all on the same page.

A theme can be the starting point for establishing your intended outcomes for the event. In my opinion, every conference, meeting and special event should have a theme and a clearly defined purpose and expressed objectives.

Your conference purpose and objectives, along with your theme, will foster a strong foundation on which to build and host an impactful event.

From years of planning all types of events with clearly defined themes, purposes and objectives, to being a part of event teams who didn't have these three essential items in place, I can unequivocally say having this trio puts you on the path to hosting a successful event.

Before I share the awesome themes presented in this book, let's take a moment and speak a little more about your conference purpose and objectives and what they look like.

"Coming together is

a beginning; keeping

together is progress;

working together

is success."

-- Henry Ford --

Chapter 2:

Clarifying

Your Conference

Purpose & Objectives

Planning and hosting a conference or special event can be exciting! With this excitement also comes the challenge of keeping your team or committee, and everyone involved, on the same page. Picking an awesome theme for your event is paramount! It's definitely a key that shouldn't be excluded from your conference planning key ring. Having a theme undoubtedly will open the door to hosting a successful conference, meeting or special event. Another key you must include on your conference planning key ring is clarifying what your conference or event purpose and objectives will be.

Pinpointing Your Purpose

In the simplest terms, your purpose helps you pinpoint your main goal for doing the event. Your purpose allows your entire event planning team to clearly formulate an answer to this question: *"Why are we having this special gathering?"* When you're clear on your purpose, you and your team can move forward with a single vision and hit the target with calculated precision.

If you desire, your purpose can be a fully composed purpose statement, but I suggest you keep it simple. Narrow your purpose or conference goal down to one to three words or a simple phrase. As you view the following list, I'm sure you can pick one to three items that sum up why you are having your conference or special event.

- To empower
- To inspire
- To inform
- To announce
- To educate
- To motivate
- To excite
- To train
- To coach
- To reconcile
- To create
- To fortify
- To build
- To heal
- To restore

- To encourage
- To have fun
- For impartation
- To restore peace
- To discuss business
- To establish new policies
- To unite or reunite
- To bring awareness
- To bring clarity
- To acknowledge/reward
- To gain ground & territory
- To build confidence
- To shift paradigms
- Team building
- Problem solving

- To introduce a person or ideology

- To pray and intercede

- To praise and worship

- To prepare for a new season

- To save and deliver

- To bring people to Christ

- To draw people closer to God

- To declare God's will and purpose

NOTES:
Use the space below to list other purposes/goals for your special event.

_____

_____

_____

_____

_____

_____

Conference Objectives

You've chosen an awesome theme and clarified your event's purpose. What's next? As you move further down the path to planning your special event, an equally important strategy is to clarify your conference or event objectives.

Basically, your objectives establish what the "take-aways" will be for your conference registrants or event attendees. Your objectives allow you and your team to pinpoint what those attending your gathering will leave with.

For example, you have decided to host an empowerment conference for families. Your theme will be: *We Are Family: Restoring the Bonds of Peace.* You and your team or committee have decided the purpose of the conference will be to empower, unite and restore peace. With those important conference elements decided, you can now establish your objectives for the event. What will be the important "take-aways" for your conference attendees? Here are a few objectives that could work for this type of gathering:

- Clarify why peace is critical in the family unit.

- Identify things that rob the family peace.

- Discuss ways to keep or restore the family peace.

- Help each family member understand their role in the family unit.

- Establish why communication is important in the family unit and explore great ways to communicate effectively to maintain peace.

Now that your conference objectives are clear, you and your team can move forward to plan the rest of your event. Having your objectives for your special gathering in clear view, you can now build upon this solid event planning foundation.

One final note about why you should add your conference purpose and objectives to your conference planning key ring. Clarifying these two important elements is crucial because it helps you and your team move forward to address the following important event planning questions:

- What type of event should we have? (More about that later)

- Who will be great speakers or experts for this event to help us fulfill our purpose and meet our objectives?

- How long should the event be? (Two hours, one day, two days, a week, etc.)

- Should we have breakout sessions to make sure we cover all our objectives?

- Can the event be done virtually or will having the event at a physical location be better?

- What's the perfect venue?

- Should the event be free or should we charge a registration fee?

- Should we have one speaker or multiple speakers?

- Should it be a morning or evening event?

- How many people should we plan for?

- Do we provide handouts?

- What's the best time of year to host our conference?

- What's the best promotional materials to use?

- How can this event be promoted on social media?

- Do we need a website specifically for this event?

And the list goes on...

Now that we have established the importance of selecting an awesome conference theme and clarifying your purpose and objectives, let's move to the next chapter and look at the different types of events you can have.

NOTES:

Use the space below to list other important event planning questions that would need to be addressed.

_____

_____

_____

_____

_____

_____

_____

_____

_____

_____

_____

_____

_____

_____

_____

_____

_____

Chapter 3:

Help!

What Type of Event

Should I Have?

When embarking upon planning a special gathering, another key element you need to decide is, "What type of event should I have?" In the world of event planning, events come in all types, shapes and sizes. Choosing the type of event that will work best depends on your target audience, the size of your audience, your theme, your purpose and your objectives.

For example, what may be conducive to reaching a smaller audience may not work for a larger audience. An event designed for youth may not be suitable for seniors. Here's one final example to consider. Perhaps your target audience is located around the globe. Instead of having a physical face-to-face gathering, like a seminar or conference, you may decide to host a virtual event such as a webinar or webcast. Or you may consider doing a combination of a face-to-face and virtual event using streaming technology.

Having a full understanding of the different types of special events you could host will add to your conference planning key ring and open doors to a multitude of effective options. Following here is a list of the types of events you can choose from.

Conference

A conference is a special gathering designed to bring a group of people with common interests together for a common purpose or cause, or to exchange ideas. The purpose of the conference will vary, but it's generally constructed to inform, empower, inspire, instruct, educate, etc. A conference can vary in size, duration and featured activities. The featured activities vary based on the theme, purpose, goals and objectives of the event.

Convention

A convention is very similar to a conference when it comes to setup and inner workings, but it may be a more formal assembly, featuring specified keynote speeches. A convention may include special delegates sent to represent a particular people group, region or cause. A convention often includes special sessions and elections to give the delegates a chance to elect their chosen representative(s).

Seminar

A seminar is an informational meeting where featured speakers cover a particular subject of interest and their target audience is invited to attend in order to be informed, empowered and educated from this exchange of ideas.

Webinar

A webinar is a virtual, online seminar where the host/speaker covers a particular subject of interest. The webinar attendees are given the opportunity to join the event via the Internet, using their computer or mobile devices from the comfort of their home or office.

Webcast

A webcast, much like a webinar, is a virtual event where the host invites registrants to view a featured speaker(s) or special event like a concert via the Internet, using their computer or mobile devices in their home, office or a specified venue capable of accommodating small or large groups of people. In the large group setting, the webcast is usually projected on a large screen. The webcast is broadcasted through streaming technology from a centralized location to people tuning in around the globe. The webcast may also include interaction between the host, speaker(s) and the virtual audience using social media outlets such as Skype, Periscope, Twitter, Facebook, etc.

Breakout

A breakout is a part of a conference where registrants are given the opportunity to break out into small group sessions. The smaller sessions are designed to offer various subjects aligned with the event objectives. These small group sessions are usually conducted concurrently to offer the conference registrants exposure to a variety of speakers and topics.

Banquet

A banquet is a formal or informal celebratory event which can include a keynote address, awards and dining. This gathering often involves recognizing an individual or cause for an achievement or significant milestone.

Luncheon

Similar to a banquet, a luncheon is a formal event held specifically during the hours lunch is served. A luncheon can include a keynote address and other special presentations. This type of gathering may be held for a number of reasons and is a great way to bring people and ideas together for fellowship, networking, inspiration and empowerment.

Retreat

A retreat is an informal gathering where the target audience is invited to get away from normal activities to focus on a particular subject of interest as presented by the retreat host and featured speakers. A retreat is also organized to be a time for registrants to rest, refresh and replenish. To accomplish this goal, specified time is normally set aside during the event for a spiritual, emotional and physical respite. A retreat is also a special event designed to help individuals, couples, families and teams regain their focus.

Intensive

Unlike a retreat, which offers a a slow-paced, low-intensity informational gathering, an intensive is a special event offering a fast-paced, high-intensity flow of information. The goal of an intensive is to empower the event registrants on a particular subject of interest in a short period of time.

Symposium

A symposium is a strategic event designed to feature various experts from different disciplines, all focusing on one particular subject of interest. The goal of a symposium is for the experts to share their expertise to inform, educate and empower the event attendees all under one roof.

Workshop

A workshop is much like a seminar. It's an event designed to inform registrants on a particular subject of interest, but it also includes giving the attendees space for hands-on activities that reinforce what was covered by the workshop facilitator. Workshops can be a great way to accelerate learning.

Advance

An advance is similar to an intensive, but the pace isn't as fast. An advance also provides a platform for industry experts to share their expertise to advance or accelerate ideas, a cause or a movement.

Roundtable

A roundtable includes a panel of invited guest speakers engaging and discussing ideas on a particular subject of interest in an open forum. This event normally includes a moderator who introduces the specified topic(s) of discussion and presents questions from the audience to the roundtable panelists.

Festival

A festival is much like a conference, but this special event is designed to offer event registrants more entertainment and empowerment options for their enjoyment and personal growth. A festival can include various main attractions such as concerts, special interest shows, exhibits, general sessions with celebrity keynotes, etc. Most festivals are designed to attract a multi-generational audience and boast of having something for everyone.

Expo

An expo is a conference designed for businesses, vendors and service providers to exhibit and expose the general public or other businesses to their products and services. The expo can also include space for industry experts to speak and introduce new trends.

Camp

A camp event is normally hosted in an outdoor setting at a campsite or retreat center. The campsite or retreat center may offer various types of accommodations such as lodges, cabins, dorms, etc. A camp event can be designed to include general sessions, breakout sessions and special outdoors and nature activities aligned with the conference theme, purpose and objectives. The camp can also include special activities such as baptisms, bonfires, prayer walks, team-building exercises, etc.

Summit

A summit is a special event designed to host heads of state and those in leadership. The event normally includes time for leaders to get away to assemble with other leaders or those in similar callings to ascend to new heights, in order to exchange ideas and decide on the next course of action.

Appreciation

An appreciation is an event designed to honor and celebrate the life and service of a person or persons being recognized. An appreciation event can be designed as a one-day observance or as a multi-day event, with different keynote speakers acknowledging the honoree and their accomplishments.

Awards Ceremony

An awards ceremony is similar to an appreciation event, but it can include recognizing and honoring multiple people based on their merit, contributions and service in various industries or genres.

Book Signing

A book signing event is a special event designed for an author to share a newly released book with their target audience. It can be a formal or informal event and normally includes the author presenting a small portion from their book to whet the appetite of potential book buyers and enthusiasts. This special event also provides space for the audience to purchase the author's new book and have it signed by the author. If applicable, the author or the event planner can use the book's title as the theme for the event or choose a theme that coincides with the subject of the book.

Teleconference

Similar to a conference, a teleconference is designed to bring a group of people with a common interest together for a common purpose or cause, or to exchange ideas. The difference is that the event is hosted in a virtual environment. The registrants are invited to experience the activities of the teleconference via the Internet using their computer or mobile devices from the comfort of their home or office. The unique aspect of this type of event is that the featured speaker is also using a computer or mobile device from the comfort of home or office to engage the audience. This type of event is cost effective because it eliminates some of the larger expenses of a face-to-face physical conference, such as renting a venue, speaker travel, etc. One point that bears mentioning: when hosting a teleconference, be sure to research the best technology to use. Some teleconference services can be problematic. Testing them out before the event is advised.

Prayer Breakfast

A prayer breakfast is a unique event that is hosted in the morning during the hours when breakfast is served. This type of event is centered around prayer and can include a keynote address and other special presentations. This type of gathering can be held for a number of reasons, but the main reason is to bring people together to orchestrate a call to prayer or launch a prayer initiative.

Chapter 4:

Leaving Your Mark:

The Power of

Conference Branding

When it comes to planning a conference or hosting a special event, branding is a key component that shouldn't be overlooked. This is especially true if you plan to host your event each year. It's important to spend considerable time and money developing a strong brand to attract your target audience as you market and promote your event in the marketplace.

Branding your event allows you to leave your mark and helps you create marketing and promotional equity that will bring you great returns each time you host your conference or special event. As you brand your event in the same way each time, it becomes recognizable in the marketplace to your target audience. They, in turn, are drawn to it and are sure to come back or register each time you host the event.

Another key reason branding your event is important is the sheer fact that there may be multiple conferences or special events in different geographical areas with the same target audience in mind, as well as the same conference title.

For example, you may have multiple conferences throughout the nation, or in a particular region, titled *Sister 2 Sister Women's Conference*. To distinguish their conference from the others in the marketplace, each conference committee must create a strong brand for their specific event.

What exactly is branding? What are the components needed to create a strong brand for your conference or special event?

Most think branding only includes creating a nice logo design for a product, service or event. But brand development includes more than that. It also includes many aspects of how your brand, or in this context, how your conference or special event is perceived by the public, especially your target audience. These aspects include:

- Your conference logo
- Typeface/fonts used
- Photos and graphics chosen
- Tag lines/Slogans
- Colors
- Your service
- Your products
- Your work ethic
- Your reputation
- The voice and message of your brand

As these items are consistently and positively displayed in the marketplace, you, your business and/or organization and your conference become known for them. If you spend considerable time, money and care developing your brand, you will have favorable outcomes when it comes to leaving a positive impression in the minds of the public at large. You, in turn, build valuable brand equity. If this is the case, you're on your way to gaining a great reputation that can easily equate to more business, greater support, greater influence, greater exposure and ultimately greater conference registrations and event attendance.

Here are things to consider when developing your conference brand:

- What is your company's or organization's message?

- What solutions will your company or organization provide through this event?

- What is your company's or organization's vision, mission and purpose for this event?

- What are the unique qualities you want the public to remember about your business or organization as a result of hosting this event?

- What are the unique features, benefits and advantages of your conference products and services?

Branding basically tells the public what they can expect from you, your business/organization, your events and your products and services.

The future of your conference, as well as your business or organization, depends on how you develop and manage your conference brand. Brand development and management, or the lack thereof, can either make or break your special event. This, in turn, can cause you to miss opportunities to use your event for God's glory and advance His agenda.

I want to highlight a perfect example of awesome conference branding. Case in point: Bishop T.D. Jakes Ministries and The Potter's House. Each year, these organizations put on wonderful conferences that empower and uplift their selected target audiences. Three conferences I personally have attended come to mind: *Woman Thou Art Loosed*, *MegaFest* and *International Pastors and Leadership Conference*.

With close examination, you will find that each of these annual conferences is branded differently. Each conference has its own individual logo design with a select use of choice typeface/fonts, colors and graphics/photos. Each conference has a different feel, voice and message geared to attract its specific target.

I've noticed Bishop Jakes and his team will choose a different theme (the centralized focus) for each of these events annually. But to help the public identify these conferences as their signature events, Team Jakes and Team Potter's House will use the established branding when marketing and promoting. They will, however, tweak the photos and graphics to flow in accordance with the selected theme.

Having attended many conferences hosted by Bishop Jakes and his team, I want to make one final observation: each conference or special event has Bishop Jakes' branded stamp of excellence. Because of this, I've come to expect that each conference or special event will deliver what is advertised, and with a spirit of excellence. In addition, I know the Spirit of God will be present. This undoubtedly keeps me and thousands of others coming back and registering each year.

Let the Planning Begin

This wraps up our discussion of the initial components needed to start planning your upcoming conference or special event. I encourage you to utilize all the keys on your conference planning key ring as discussed and let the planning begin!

But before you start planning, I want to encourage you not to box the Holy Spirit in when it comes to planning your event. Please be open to the creative flow of ideas He will inspire you with and lead you to do. I also encourage you not to get caught up in focusing on your personal agenda and hosting an event only to impress men. Because when all is said and done, the bottom line when hosting Spirit-led events is to bring God glory and fulfill His agenda.

Chapter 5:

Finding Your Theme:

How the Themes Are

Organized

To make it easy for you to find the perfect theme for your special event, this book has been alphabetically arranged into categories. The categories are based on your target audience or the kind of ideas you want to convey. The categories include themes that are geared toward a particular people group (men, women, youth, singles, etc.) or themes that focus on a particular subject such as leadership, finance, marriage, empowerment, prayer, Kingdom Dominion, etc.

Another important organization note worth mentioning: as I was writing the themes, compiling the list and creating the categories, I noticed that some themes could be used for more than one particular people group or subject. I decided to include multi-functional categories that combined certain people groups and subjects.

For example, the conference theme *Divine Coverings: The Power of Kingdom Protocol* would make an awesome theme for a leadership conference, but it would also work well as a theme for a marriage empowerment conference. So the multi-functional category was listed as "Leadership, Marriage Empowerment."

Here's another example. The conference theme *Empowered to Possess: Living Life Without Limits* is an awesome conference theme that could be used for a conference geared toward women and men. You could also use this theme for a conference that focuses on Kingdom Dominion. This theme would also work for an empowerment conference! So to help you see all the possibilities for this particular theme, I created a category called "Women, Men, Kingdom Dominion, Empowerment."

As you dive into this resource, you will see how the themes can serve different target audiences and subjects. Let's look at what type of categories made the list.

Appreciation, Anniversary, Awards

Arts, Drama

Empowerment

Empowerment, Inner Healing

Empowerment, Prophetic, Kingdom Dominion

Evangelism, Missions

Family and Friends Day, Marriage Empowerment

Family Empowerment

Father's Day, Men

Finance, Business, Leadership, Empowerment

General, Corporate

Inner Healing

Kingdom Dominion, Prophetic

Leadership

Leadership, Business

Leadership, Business, Men

Leadership, Business, Women

Leadership, Kingdom Dominion, Empowerment

Leadership, Marriage Empowerment

Marriage Empowerment

Men

Men, Father's Day

Ministry of Helps

Praise, Worship, Arts, Music

Prayer, Intercession, Spiritual Warfare

Prophetic

Seniors

Singles

Women

Women, Men, Kingdom Dominion, Empowerment

Women, Mother's Day

Youth, Young Adult

Final Note

One final note concerning how the book is organized. To make it easy for you to find an awesome theme for your event, you can use the Table of Contents, which leads you directly to where a particular category listing can be found in the book. If you choose to just thumb through the book, you will also find the categories listed at the top of each page in the header. Happy theme picking!

Man of Destiny: A Father to the Nations

Woman of Destiny: A Mother to the Nations

Yielded to Serve: A Legacy Remembered

Legacy Living: Honoring a Father of Zion

Legacy Living: Honoring a Mother of Zion

Standing Tall Through It All

Still Standing

Still Standing: Upon Your Shoulders We Rise

Created to Create: We Bring Our Gifts to You

Created to Create: Glorious Expressions of Praise

Created to Create: Submitted to Service

Creatively Endowed: We Submit Our Hearts to You

Creatively Endowed: My Gift, His Glory

Creatively Endowed: My Gift, His Voice

Dance Warriors: A Force to Be Reckoned With

Dance Warriors: Releasing the Heavenlies

Dance Warriors: Taking Dominion

Dance Warriors: Moving the Heavens, Shaking the Earth

Dance Warriors: Creating a Glorious Flow

Dance Warriors: In Step for Dominion

Dancing with Purpose: Our Worship, His Presence

Dancing with Purpose: Moving the Hand of God

Dancing with Purpose: Calling Forth the Miraculous

Aspire to Inspire: Empowering the Next Generation

Aspire to Inspire: Empowering People for Change

Aspire to Inspire: Mentoring the Next Generation

Breakthrough: Embracing the Promises of God

Breakthrough: Stepping into the Overflow

Breakthrough: Strategies for Success

Breakthrough: Living Life Without Limits

Dimensional Shifts to Success

Dimensional Shifts: Stepping into Greatness

Dare to Believe: Soaring to New Heights

Dare to Believe: Living Life Without Limits

Dare to Believe: Stepping into the Next Dimension

Positioned to Transition: Moving Beyond the Past

Positioned for Possession: Stepping into Greatness

Positioned for Possession: Moving Beyond Fear

Positioned for Possession: Moving Beyond Uncertainty

Positioned for Possession: Entering into New Territory

Positioned for Possession: Crossing Over into Destiny

Positioned for Possession: Living Life Without Limits

Positioned for Possession: Living Life Without Boundaries

Positioned for Possession: Living Life to the Fullest

Positioned for Possession: Moving Beyond the Past

Breakthrough: Stepping into Greatness

Called to Conquer: Raising from the Rubbles

Dare to Believe: Maximized Living

Rekindling the Passion

Rekindling the Passion for God

Rekindling the Passion for Ministry

Rekindling the Passion for the Word

Rekindling the Passion for Life

Restoring the Drive for Ministry

Restoring the Hunger for the Word

Restoring the Hunger for Righteousness

Restoring the Hunger for God

Success Ahead - Exit Right: Strategies for Moving Forward

Success Ahead - Exit Right: Moving Beyond the Past

Positioned to Transition: Moving Beyond the Past

Positioned to Transition: Stepping into Greatness

Positioned to Transition: Moving Beyond Fear

Positioned to Transition: Moving Beyond Uncertainty

Positioned to Transition: Entering into New Territory

Positioned to Transition: Crossing Over into Destiny

Positioned to Transition: Living Life Without Limits

Positioned to Transition: Living Life Without Boundaries

Positioned for Possession: Moving Beyond Doubt

Positioned to Transition: Living Life to the Fullest

Breakthrough: Living Life Without Boundaries

Breakthrough: Stepping into Greatness

Breakthrough: Moving Beyond Fear

Breakthrough: Moving Beyond Uncertainty

Breakthrough: Entering into New Territory

Breakthrough: Crossing Over into Destiny

Breakthrough: Living Life Without Limits

Breakthrough: Living Life Without Boundaries

Breakthrough: Living Life to the Fullest

Dimensional Shifts: Stepping into the Promise

Dimensional Shifts to Uplift

Divine Conceptions: Birthing the Promises of God

Divine Conceptions: Birthing Your Dreams and Visions

Divine Dispositions: Postured to Possess the Promise

Empowered to Possess God's Best

Empowered to Possess

Empowered to Possess the Promise

Empowered to Prosper

In Tune with Success

In Tune with Destiny

Kingdom Paradigms: Training for Reigning

Kingdom Paradigms: Walking in Dominion

Kingdom Paradigms: Sons of God Revealed

Kingdom Paradigms: Shifting into the Next Dimension

Kingdom Paradigms: Embracing Divine Thought Patterns

Manifested: Empowered to Possess

Maximized Mind-shifts

Beyond Walls: A Call to Reach the Nations

Dare to Believe: Taking the Nations for Christ

Empowered to Reach the Nations

Energized to Evangelize

Energized to Evangelize: Reaching the Hearts of the Community

Energized to Evangelize: Reaching the Nations for Christ

United to Heal - United to Build

United to Love: Building Bridges of Hope

United to Give: Building Bridges of Hope

Energized to Evangelize: Building Bridges of Hope

Called to Serve: The Power of Servanthood

Commissioned to Missions: Winning the Nations to Christ

Commissioned to Missions: Captivating the Nations

Commissioned to Missions: Moving Beyond Our Borders

Commissioned to Missions: Winning the Lost to Christ

Commissioned to Missions: Taking Christ to the Nations

Commissioned to Missions: Empowering the Nations for Christ

Commissioned to Missions: Uniting the Nations for Christ

Commissioned to Missions: Global Impact

Commissioned to Missions: Restoring the Nations

Commissioned to Missions: Lifting Up a Standard for Christ

Commissioned to Missions: Taking the Nations for Christ

Commissioned to Missions: A United Front

Commissioned to Missions: Global Initiatives for Change

Commissioned to Missions: Global Initiatives for Christ

Commissioned to Missions: Tearing Down Barriers
of Religion

Commissioned to Missions: Reaching Our Community for Christ

Joined to Impact: Restoring the Bonds of Peace

Joined to Impact: Standing Strong and United

United to Stand: Restoring the Bonds of Peace

United to Stand: Creating an Atmosphere for Change

The Call: United Globally

The Call: Fulfilling God's Will on the Earth

The Call: Filling the Earth with the Glory of God

The Call: Reaching a Generation for Christ

The Call: Reaching the World for Christ

The Call: Winning the Nations to Christ

The Call: Captivating the Nations

The Call: Moving Beyond Our Borders

The Call: Tearing Down Barriers of Religion

The Call: Winning the Lost to Christ

The Call: Taking Christ to the Nations

The Call: Empowering the Nations for Christ

The Call: Uniting the Nations for Christ

The Call: Global Impact

The Call: Restoring the Nations

The Call: Lifting Up a Standard for Christ

The Call: Taking the Nations for Christ

The Call: A United Front

The Call: Global Initiatives for Change

The Call: Global Initiatives for Christ

The Call: Fulfilling the Great Commission

The Call: Reaching Our Community for Christ

The Call: Reaching Our Nation for Christ

Word Domination: Taking God's Word to the Nations

Word Domination: Proclaiming the Gospel to the Nations

Word Domination: A Call to Discipleship

Word Domination: The Power of God's Word

Word Domination: Captivated by the Gospel

Word Domination: The Power of the Gospel Declared

Joined Impact: A Global Initiative for Christ

Commissioned to Submission: A Call to Greatness

Commissioned to Submission: Serving on Christ's Behalf

Commissioned to Submission: A Call to Serve

Commissioned to Submission: Access to Greatness

Commissioned to Submission: The Power of Servant Leadership

Commissioned to Submission: The Power of Servanthood

Joined to Impact: Reaching the Nations for Christ

Joined to Impact: A United Commission for Change

Joined to Impact: Reaching the Nations for Christ

United to Stand: A Global Initiative for Christ

Kingdom Connections: Tearing Down the Barrier of Religion

We Are Family: United to Impact

We Are Family: Repairing the Breach

We Are Family: Building Stronger Connections

We Are Family: Empowered to Impact

We Are Family: A House Undivided

We Are Family: Raising a Standard for Christ

We Are Family: Restoring the Bond

We Are Family: Breaking Down Barriers

We Are Family: Restoring the Bonds of Peace

We Are Family: Reaching the Family for Christ

We Are Family: Reaching a Generation for Christ

We Are Family: Reaching Youth for Christ

We Are Family: Building a Stronger Tomorrow

We Are Family: A United Stand for Change

We Are Family: A United Commission for Change

We Are Family: The Power of Agreement

Family First: The Power of Covenant Relationships

Family First: Standing Strong Together

Family First: Creating an Atmosphere for Change

Family First: Restoring Relationships

Family First: Mending the Broken Heart

Family First: Mending the Connection

Family First: Building a Bridge for Change

Family First: United to Impact

Welcome Home: Our Doors are Open

Welcome Home: A Place to Find Peace

Welcome Home: A Refuge from the Storm

Welcome Home: Let the Celebration Begin

Welcome Home: Your Place Is Here

Welcome Home: Your Resting Place

Welcome Home: It's Family Time

Welcome Home: A Call to Restoration

Welcome Home: United by Love

Welcome Home: United in Love

United to Stand: Standing Strong Together

United to Stand: Reaching the Community for Christ

United to Stand: Lifting Up a Standard for Christ

United to Stand: A Call for Change

United to Stand: A House Built Upon a Solid Foundation

United to Stand: A Call for Love

United to Stand: A Church Without Walls

United to Stand: A Community Without Walls

United to Stand: A Call for Peace

United to Heal - United to Build

United to Love: Building Bridges of Hope

United to Love: Restoring the Bonds of Peace

Standing Tall Through It All

Standing Tall Together: Building Community and Unity

Joined to Impact

Joined to Impact: Restoring the Bond

Joined to Impact: Raising a Standard for Christ

Joined to Impact: Breaking Down Barriers

Joined to Impact: A Positive Initiative for Change

Joined to Impact: Reaching the Family for Christ

Joined to Impact: A United Stand

Joined to Impact: A United Stand for Change

Joined to Impact: The Power of Agreement

Joined to Impact: The Power of Covenant Relationships

Joined to Impact: Standing Strong Together

Joined to Impact: Lifting Up a Standard for Christ

Joined to Impact: A Call for Change

Joined to Impact: A Call for Peace

Joined to Impact: A House Undivided

Joined to Impact: A Call for Love

United to Stand: A House Undivided

United to Stand: Restoring the Bond

United to Stand: Raising a Standard for Christ

United to Stand: Breaking Down Barriers

United to Stand: A Positive Initiative for Change

United to Stand: Reaching Every Generation

United to Stand: Building a Stronger Tomorrow

United to Stand: Covenants for Change

United to Stand: A United Commission for Change

United to Stand: The Power of Agreement

United to Stand: The Power of Covenant Relationships

A Call to Excellence: Families Lifting Up a Standard

Aspire to Inspire: Mentoring the Next Generation

Ascend to Defend: Fathers Rising Up to Preserve the
Next Generation

Ascend to Defend: Husbands Taking Their Place
in the Marriage

Reverse the Curse: Overcoming Generational Curses

Breakthrough: Overcoming Generational Curses

Breakthrough: Possessing the Promises of God

Building Strong Families for Christ

Divine Dispositions: Postured to Possess the Promise

Divine Dispositions: Postured for Generational Blessings

We Are Family: United to Impact

We Are Family: Empowered to Impact

A Body of One: United to Impact

Family First: United to Impact

United to Heal - United to Build

United to Love: Building Bridges of Hope

United to Give: Building Bridges of Hope

Empowered to Parent Positively

Divine Conceptions: Raising Godly Children

Joined Impact: Reaching the Family for Christ

Welcome Home: A Sanctuary of Love

Welcome Home: A Place for You

Welcome Home: A Place for Renewal

Welcome Home: Breaking Down the Barriers

Welcome Home: United to Serve Christ

Welcome Home: Closer than Ever

Welcome Home: Building a Family Bond

Successful Succession: Preparing the Next Generation to Prosper

Successful Succession: Leading by Example

Successful Succession: From Destiny to Dynasty

Successful Succession: Creating a Divine Dynasty

Successful Succession: Equipping the Next Generation

Raising the Standard: When Godly Parents Lead

Ascend to Defend: Fathers Taking Their Place in the Family

Leading the Way: Fathers Called to Serve

Legends in the Making

Man of Destiny: A Father to the Generations

Men of Honor: A Force to be Reckoned With

Men of Honor: Lifting Up a Standard

Men of Valor: Called to Serve Our Family

Men of Valor: Raising the Standard

Men of Valor: Lifting Up a Standard

Men of Strength and Power: Lifting Up a Standard

Men on the Front Line: Lifting Up a Standard

Men on the Front Line: Standing Strong

Men on the Front Line: Called to Impact the Next Generation

Men on the Front Line: Fortified to Fight

Men on the Front Line: Armed and Dangerous

Men on the Front Line: Called to Conquer

Mighty Men of Valor: Raising the Standard

Mighty Men of Valor: Called to Honor

Mighty Men of Valor: Called to Serve

Mighty Men of Valor: Called to Defend

Paradigms from the Top: Learning from the Legends

Paradigms from the Top: Learning from the Masters

Paradigms from the Top: Cultivating Divine Mentalities

Postured for Possession: Embracing My Divine Inheritance

Postured for Possession: Sowing into My Future

Postured for Possession: Laying Hold of the Promise

Released to Increase: Living in the Overflow

Rewired for Wealth

Rewired for Wealth: Shifting Your Financial Paradigms

Rewired for Wealth: Changing Your Family Tree

Rewired for Wealth: New Paradigms, New Opportunities

Rewired for Wealth: Divine Calculations

In Sync with Success: My Time Is Now

In Sync with Success: Positioned to Prosper

In Sync with Success: Living in Beat with God's Purpose

In Sync with Success: Mastering the Moment

In Sync with Success: Possessing the Promises of God

In Sync with Success: Seizing My Season

Living in the Overflow

Living in the Overflow: Living Life Without Limits

Living in the Overflow: Living Life Without Boundaries

Living in the Overflow: Living Life to the Fullest

Living in the Overflow: Breaking Down Barriers

Breakthrough: Stepping into the Overflow

Empowered to Prosper

Empowered to Prosper: Blessed to Be a Blessing

Maximized Mind-shifts: Thinking Like God

Maximized Mind-shifts: Mastering Your Money

Maximized Mind-shifts: Embracing Paradigms for Success

Maximized Mind-shifts: A View from the Top

Maximized Mind-shifts: Moving to the Next Dimension

The Ingathering of the God's Elect: Together We Stand

The Ingathering of the God's Elect: Unified to Conquer

The Power of One: Corporate Impact

The Power of One: Unified to Conquer

A Body of One: United to Impact

Divine Connections - Corporate Blessings

United to Impact: The Power of Covenant Relationships

Corporate Alliances: United to Impact

Corporate Alliances: Strength in Numbers

The Corporate Collective: United to Stand

The Corporate Collective: United to Empower

United to Heal - United to Build

United to Love: Building Bridges of Hope

United to Give: Building Bridges of Hope

Rekindling the Passion

Rekindling the Flames of the Spirit

Beyond Yesterday: Healing the Wounded Heart

Beyond Yesterday: My Pain, His Promise

Breakthrough: Moving Beyond the Past

Breakthrough: Freedom Beyond the Pain

The Great Exchange: Beauty for Ashes

The Great Exchange: A New Creature for Christ

The Great Exchange: My Pain, His Promise

The Great Exchange: Entering the New

Licensed to Live: Breakthrough to Victory

Licensed to Live: Overcoming the Pain

Licensed to Live: Overcoming the Obstacles

Renewed: Moving Beyond the Past

Renewed: Energized to Live

Refueled: Moving Beyond the Past

Refueled: Energized to Live

Access Granted: Stepping into the Next Dimension

Ascend to Defend: Men Taking Their Place in the Kingdom

Dare to Believe: Soaring to New Heights

Divine Conceptions: The Birthing of a Nation

Divine Conceptions: The Birthing of the Manifested Sons of God

Divine Dispositions: Postured to Possess the Kingdom

From Revelation to Manifestation

From Revelation to Manifestation: Giving Birth to Spiritual Realities

Glory Arise: Embracing the Manifested Presence of God

Kingdom Paradigms: Sons of God Revealed

Locked and Loaded: Moving in Kingdom Authority

Men Empowered for Kingdom Dominion

No Limits: Possessing the Promises of the Kingdom

No Limits: Stepping into Kingdom Dominion

No Limits: Walking in the Fullness of the Promise

Open Hearts, Open Heavens

Positioned to Transition

PUSH: Birthing a Nation of Warriors

PUSH: Birthing a People Called to Purpose

Shekinah Glory: Embracing the Manifested Presence of God

Shekinah Glory: God Revealed

Shekinah Glory: Abiding in the Secret Place

Shekinah Glory: Seated in Heavenly Places

Shekinah Glory: Open Hearts, Open Heavens

Women Empowered for Kingdom Dominion

Divine Conceptions: Planting Seeds of Heaven on Earth

Divine Conceptions: Birthing the Purposes of God

Divine Conceptions: Giving Birth to Destiny

Divine Conceptions: Living in the Secret Place

Divine Dispositions: Postured to Possess the Kingdom

Divine Dispositions: Postured to Reach the Nations

Kingdom Paradigms: Sons of God Manifested

Kingdom Paradigms: Sons of God Revealed

Unveiled: Manifesting Kingdom Authority

Open Hearts, Open Heavens

Manifested: Fulfilling God's Covenant in the Earth

Heads of State: Lifting Up a Standard of Righteousness

Heads of State: Raising Up Effective Leaders

Heads of State: Leading the Next Generation

Heads of State: Mentoring for the Next Move of God

Heads of State: Strategic Positioning for the Future

Heads of State: Fulfilling the Mandate to Lead

Heads of State: Raising the Bar for Righteousness

Heads of State: Leading with the Heart of God

Heads of State: Advancing God's Agenda in the Earth

Heads of State: Servant Leadership that Glorifies God

Aspire to Inspire: Setting the Standard for
the Next Generation

Divine Coverings: Aligned for Purpose and Promotion

Ecclesiastical Commissions: Preparing the Body of Christ
to Serve

Ecclesiastical Commissions: Leaders Called to Serve the Body

Ecclesiastical Commissions: Fulfilling the Purpose of God

Ecclesiastical Commissions: Serving the Kingdom

Successful Succession: Preparing the Leaders of Tomorrow

Successful Succession: Mentoring the Leaders of Tomorrow

Ecclesiastical Commissions: Leaders Impacting the Nations

Aspire to Inspire: Mentoring the Next Generation

Called and Chosen: Raising Up a Joshua Company

Divine Conceptions: Giving Birth to Godly Visions

Heads of State: Leading the Way to Future Innovations

Leaders in the Making: Trained to Reign

Leading the Way: Innovations for a Brighter Day

Leading the Way: Leaders Called to Serve

Leading the Way: Mentors Called to Serve

Legends in the Making

Paradigms from the Top

Paradigms from the Top: Learning from the Legends

Paradigms from the Top: Gaining the Mastery

Paradigms from the Top: Positioned to Transition

Paradigms from the Top: Postured for Possession

PUSH: Birthing Dreams and Visions

PUSH: Birthing the Purposes of God

PUSH: Birthing Your Destiny

Raising the Standard: When Godly Leaders Lead

Successful Succession: Leaders in the Making

Successful Succession: Preparing the Leaders of Tomorrow

Successful Succession: Preparing the Next Generation for Marketplace Ministry

Successful Succession: Preparing the Next Generation to Win

Breakfast of Champions: Power Up

Breakfast of Champions: United to Impact

Plugged In: Powered up to Prosper

Plugged In: The Power of Synergetic Relationships

Called and Chosen: Nurturing Leaders for the Next Dimension

Called and Chosen: Leaders Standing Strong

Called and Chosen: Christian Leaders in the Marketplace

Called and Chosen: A Season of Manifestation

Raising the Standard: When Godly Men Lead

Raising the Standard: When Men Stand Up, Boys Sit Down

Leading the Way: Businessmen Called to Serve

Men on the Front Line: A Call to Action

Men on the Front Line: Standing Strong

Men on the Front Line: Armed and Dangerous

Men on the Forefront: Fortified to Build

Men on the Forefront: Called to Conquer

Men on the Cutting Edge: Lifting Up a Standard

Men on the Cutting Edge: Called to Impact the
Next Generation

Men of Valor Prevail

Men of Valor Leading the Way

Mighty Men of Valor: Raising the Standard

Mighty Men of Valor: Called to Honor

Mighty Men of Valor: Called to Serve

Mighty Men of Valor: Called to Defend

Women of Destiny: A Call to Lead

Women of Destiny: Called to Serve

Women of Destiny: Balanced and Prospering

Women on the Forefront: Called to Conquer

Women on the Forefront: A Call to Action

Women on the Cutting Edge: Lifting Up a Standard

Women on the Cutting Edge: Standing Strong

Women on the Cutting Edge: Called to Impact the
Next Generation

Women on the Cutting Edge: Shattering the Glass Ceiling

The Great Reveal: Women Empowered to Lead

The Great Reveal: Women Focused on Innovation

The Great Reveal: Calling Forth Women of Destiny

The Great Reveal: Women Who Lead Well

The Great Reveal: Business Women Stepping Out of
the Shadows

The Great Reveal: Business Women Stepping Out of the Box

A Call to Excellence: Living to Bring God Glory

In Tune With Success

The Gathering of Eagles: Establishing Divine Order

The Gathering of Eagles: Moving into the Next Dimension

The Gathering of Eagles: Stepping into the Next Dimension

The Gathering of Eagles: The Power of Synergy

The Gathering of Eagles: Soaring to New Heights

The Gathering of Eagles: A Global Initiative for Change

The Gathering of Eagles: A United Stand

The Gathering of Eagles: A United Stand for Change

The Gathering of Eagles: A United Commission for Change

The Gathering of Eagles: The Power of Agreement

The Gathering of Eagles: The Power of Covenant Relationships

The Gathering of Eagles: Standing Strong Together

Gathering of the Elect: Standing Strong and United

Gathering of the Elect: Reaching the Nations for Christ

Gathering of the Elect: Lifting Up a Standard for Christ

Gathering of the Elect: Shifting into Power

Gathering of the Elect: A Leadership Initiative

Gathering of the Elect: Power Summit

Gathering of the Elect: The Convergence of Power and Authority

Gathering of the Elect: Tearing Down Barriers

Gathering of the Elect: Taking Authority for Christ

Convergence: A Global Initiative for Change

Convergence: A United Stand

Convergence: A United Stand for Change

Convergence: A United Commission for Change

Convergence: Standing Strong Together

Convergence: Standing Strong and United

Convergence: Lifting Up a Standard for Christ

Convergence: Reaching the Nations for Christ

Convergence: Shifting into Power

Convergence: A Leadership Initiative

Convergence: Power Summit for Change

Convergence: Conquering Mountains Together

Convergence: The Power of Synergistic Relationships

Convergence: Power Summit for Peace

Convergence: The Power of Synergy

A Call to Excellence: Setting the Standard for Christ

A Call to Excellence: An Open Display of His Glory

A Call to Excellence: Living by God's Principles

Aspire to Inspire: The Older Mentoring the Younger

Aspire to Inspire: Touching Lives for His Glory

Aspire to Inspire: Impacting the Next Generation

Aspire to Inspire: Living to Leave a Legacy

Kingdom Connections: Building Covenant Relationships

Kingdom Connections: Postured for Divine Alignment

Kingdom Connections: United to Empower

Postured for Possession: Seeking the Kingdom, Manifesting the Promise

Unveiled: Manifesting Kingdom Authority

Divine Coverings: The Power of Kingdom Protocol

Divine Coverings: Flowing in Perfect Alignment

Divine Coverings: Honoring the Plan of God

Divine Coverings: Establishing a Protocol for Blessings

Divine Coverings: From Submission to Commission

Joined to Impact: When We Come Together

Joined to Impact: Couples Standing as One

United to Love

United to Love: Couples Standing as One

United to Give: Building Bridges of Hope

An Intimate Affair: When Our Hearts Meet

An Intimate Affair: Rekindling the Flame

An Intimate Affair: Rekindling the Fire

An Intimate Affair: A Time to Reconnect

The Power of One: Singleness of Heart

The Two Shall Become One

Convergence: The Power of Agreement

Convergence: The Power of Covenant Relationships

Reunited: Recovering from Emotional Bankruptcy

Reunited: Restoring the Bonds of Marriage

Reunited: Captivating the Heart Again

Reunited: Moving Beyond the Pain

Reunited: The Two Shall Be One

Reunited: The Power of One

Reunited: Restoring the Passion of the Heart

Reunited: Strengthening What God Has Joined Together

Reunited: Let No Man Put Asunder

Reunited: Captivated by Your Love

Reunited: Encounters of Love

Reunited: Moving Beyond the Barriers

Married & Consecrated: A Vow to Serve

Married & Consecrated: A Vow to Honor

Married & Consecrated: Honoring Our Covenant

Married & Consecrated: Honoring the Lord in Unity

Married & Consecrated: United to Honor God

Married & Consecrated: A Vow to Uphold Purity

Married & Consecrated: Our Commitment to Covenant

Married & Consecrated: Honoring Our Covenant Before God

An Intimate Affair: Rekindling the Passion

Rekindling the Flames of Love

Manifest: When Men Reveal God's Greatness

Manifest: Empowered to Possess

A Call to Excellence: Men Lifting Up a Standard

Aspire to Inspire: Mentoring the Next Generation

Ascend to Defend: Fathers Taking Their Place in the Family

Ascend to Defend: Husbands Taking Their Place in the Marriage

Ascend to Defend: Men Taking Their Place in the Kingdom

Ascend to Defend: Men Raising to Preserve the Next Generation

Leading the Way: Fathers Called to Serve

Men Empowered for Kingdom Dominion

Men Lifting Up a Standard

Men of Distinction

Men of Distinction: Your Time Has Come

The Breakfast of Champions: When Real Men Rise

Men of Valor: Called to Serve

Men of Valor: Raising the Standard

When Men Stand Up, Boys Sit Down

Men of Honor: A Force to be Reckoned With

Men in the Combat Zone: Fighting on Our Knees

Men in the Combat Zone: Armed and Dangerous

Men in the Combat Zone: Called to Conquer

Mighty Men of Valor: Raising the Standard

Mighty Men of Valor: Called to Serve

Mighty Men of Valor: Called to Defend

Leading the Way: Honorable Men Called to Serve

The Great Reveal: Calling Forth Men of Distinction

The Great Reveal: Releasing the King in Me

The Great Reveal: Men Reflecting God's Image

Guys' Night Out: Relax and Refuel

Guys' Night Out: Strengthen and Recharge

MEN

A Few Good Men: Going Beyond the Call of Duty

A Few Good Men: Taking a Stand Together

Positioned to Protect: When Praying Men Rise

Men of Valor: Called to Serve Their Families

A Call to Excellence: Men Lifting Up a Standard

Leading the Way: Businessmen Called to Serve

Men of Destiny: Arise and Serve

Men of Distinction: Leaving a Godly Legacy

Men of Distinction: Leaving a Legacy for the Next Generation

Men of Valor: A Force to be Reckoned With

Men of Honor: Raising the Standard

Men of Strength and Power: Raising the Standard

Men of Strength and Power: Lifting Up a Standard

Men of Valor: Lifting Up a Standard

Men of Honor: Lifting Up a Standard

Men on the Front Line: A Call to Action

Men on the Front Line: Standing Strong

Men on the Front Line: Called to Impact the Next Generation

Men on the Front Line: Fortified to Fight

Mighty Men of Valor: Arise to Honor

Mentoring Fathers: Leading the Way to Godliness

Mentoring Fathers: Establishing a Legacy of Righteousness

Mentoring Fathers: Raising Up Sons for the Kingdom

Mentoring Fathers: Nurturing the Next Generation

Mentoring Fathers: Teaching by Example

Mentoring Fathers: Raising Sons of Thunder

Willing Workers: Called to Serve

Willing Workers: Commissioned for the Mission

Willing Workers: United to Build the Body

Willing Workers: Consecrated for Service

Willing Workers: Aligned with the Vision of the House

Willing Workers: Motivated to Move

Situated to Serve: Building for the Kingdom

Situated to Serve: Making an Impact for God's Glory

Situated to Serve: When We All Unite

Situated to Serve: Commissioned for the Mission

Situated to Serve: United to Build the Body

Situated to Serve: Aligned with the Vision of the House

Situated to Serve: When We All Work Together

Situated to Serve: The Body United

Situated to Serve and Motivated to Move

Unified to Glorify: When We All Work Together

Unified to Glorify: Establishing God's Kingdom on Earth

Unified to Glorify: Aligned with the Vision of the House

Unified to Glorify: Consecrated for His Purpose

Unified to Glorify: Consecrated for the Master's Use

Unified to Glorify: Aligned with the Vision of the House

Unified to Glorify: One Vision, One Purpose

Connected to Impact: When Every Joint Supplies

Connected to Impact: I Need You to Survive

Connected to Impact: Building the Wall Together

Connected to Impact: Body of Christ Unite

Connected to Impact: Aligned with the Vision of the House

Connected to Impact: When God's People See Eye-to-Eye

Breakthrough: Releasing the Dance Warrior in Me

Breakthrough: Releasing the Worship Warriors

In His Presence: A Call to Worship

Kingdom-Minded Minstrels: In Tune to Impact

Kingdom-Minded Minstrels: Releasing a Certain Sound

Kingdom-Minded Minstrels: Releasing the Clarion Call

Minstrels Releasing a Certain Sound

Minstrels Releasing the Breaker's Anointing

Minstrels with a Heart for Worship

Minstrels Empowered with Praise

Minstrels with a Message

Warrior Worshipers: Calling Forth the Heavenlies

Warrior Worshipers: Open Hearts, Open Heavens

Warrior Worshipers: Submitted to Fight

Warrior Worshipers: Invoking the Presence of God

Warrior Worshipers: Summoned to Glorify God

United in Praise

United in Praise: Submitted to Worship

United in Praise: Committed to Worship

United in Praise: Lifting Up the Name of Jesus

United in Praise: Connected by Worship

United in Praise: Declaring the Song of the Redeemed

United in Praise: Declaring the Song of the Lord

United in Praise: Declaring the Heavenly on Earth

United in Praise: Connected by Worship

United in Praise: Building a House of Worship

True Worshipers: Abiding in the Presence of God

True Worshipers: Abiding in Spirit and Truth

True Worshipers: At the Feet of the Master

True Worshipers: Broken to Serve the Master

True Worshipers: Living a Lifestyle of Submission

True Worshipers: The Great Exchange

True Worshipers: Bring Forth Pure Praise

True Worshipers: Seeking the Face of God

True Worshipers: Hungry for His Presence

True Worshipers: Releasing the Glory of God

True Worshipers: Pressing into His Presence

Perpetual Praise: Abiding in the Presence of the Almighty

Perpetual Praise: Cultivating a Heart for God

Perpetual Praise: Drawing Near unto the Father

Perpetual Praise: Presenting a Sweet-Smelling Fragrance

Perpetual Praise: Declaring God's Mighty Acts

Perpetual Praise: United as One Voice

Perpetual Praise: Abiding in the Presence of God

In Step to Impact

Dancing to Impact

Our Dance Before the King

Licensed to Live: Driven to Walk in Obedience

Licensed to Live: Driven to Serve God

In His Presence: A Call to Worship

In His Presence: Seeking the Face of God

In His Presence: Lord, Show Us Your Glory

In His Presence: We Bring Our Worship

In His Presence: An Audience with the King

Warrior Worshipers: A Force to be Reckoned With

The Great Exchange: Moving Beyond the Past

The Ascension: Stepping into the Next Dimension

The Ascension: Lord, Show Us Your Glory

The Ascension: Experiencing the Manifested Presence of God

The Ascension: A Call To Worship

The Ascension: Showers of Glory

In the Secret Place: Intimate Worship and Personal Praise

In the Secret Place: Worshiping at the Throne of God

In the Secret Place: My Worship, His Glory

Access Granted: Stepping into the Next Dimension

Armed and Dangerous

Armed and Dangerous: Locked and Loaded

Armed and Dangerous: Strategies to Defeat the Enemy

Ascend to Defend

Ascend to Defend: Prayer Warriors Taking Their Place in the Kingdom

Breakthrough: Going Behind Enemy Lines

Breakthrough: Overcoming Generational Curses

Breakthrough: Overcoming the Tactics of the Enemy

Breakthrough: Possessing the Gates of the Enemy

Breakthrough: Prayer Strategies for the Overcomer

Breakthrough: Releasing the Breaker's Anointing

Breakthrough: Setting the Captive Free

Breakthrough: Stepping into the Next Dimension

Breakthrough: When People Unite to Pray

Called to Conquer

Called to Conquer: When Men and Women Pray

Called to Conquer: United to Pray

Divine Dispositions: Postured to Possess the Promise

Dressed to Possess: Armed for Battle

Dressed to Possess: Putting on the Whole Armor of God

Fit to Fight: Armed for Battle

In His Presence: A Call to Prayer

Locked and Loaded: Moving in Kingdom Authority

Locked and Loaded: Possessing the Gates of the Enemy

Locked and Loaded: Positioned to Protect

Locked and Loaded: Postured for Prayer

Locked and Loaded: Armed for Battle

Locked and Loaded: Fighting on My Knees

Possessing the Gates of the Enemy Through Prayer

Positioned to Protect: Fighting on Our Knees

PUSH: Birthing Dimensional Anointings

Reverse the Curse: Overcoming Generational Curses

Postured for Prayer

The Breaker's Anointing: Called to Conquer

The Breaker's Anointing: Setting the Captive Free

Unveiled: Manifesting Kingdom Authority

Men in the Combat Zone: Fighting on Our Knees

Men in the Combat Zone: Called to Conquer

Women in the Combat Zone: Fighting on Our Knees

Women in the Combat Zone: Called to Conquer

Mighty Men of Valor: Raising the Prayer Standard

Mighty Men of Valor: Called to Pray and Recover All

Mighty Men of Valor: Called to Defend

Invading the Territory of the Enemy

Possessing the Gates of the Enemy

Divine Dispositions: Postured to Possess the Promise

On Guard: Positioned to Protect

On Guard: Watchmen Positioned on the Wall

Open Heavens: Stepping Behind the Veil

Open Heavens: Moving from Glory to Glory

Open Heavens: Tapping into the Realms of the Supernatural

Open Heavens: Accessing Supernatural Portals of God

Open Heavens: At the Throne of God

Open Heavens: Access Granted

Open Heavens: Developing a Culture of Intimacy

Open Heavens: Ascending on High

Open Heavens: Engaging the Throne of Heaven

Open Heavens: Accessing the Spiritual Portals

Open Heavens: At the Feet of God

Open Heavens: Accessing the Realms of Glory

Open Heavens: The Door is Open

Open Heavens: Quantum Leaps Into God's Glory

Open Heavens: The Call to Come Up Higher

The Ascension: The Door Is Opened

The Ascension: A Call to Come Up Higher

Living in the Secret Place

Living in the Secret Place: Seeking the Face of God

Living in the Secret Place: Hearing the Heartbeat of God

Living in the Secret Place: Impartations of His Glory

Living in the Secret Place: Stepping into the Next Dimension

In the Secret Place: Capturing the Heart of God

In the Secret Place: Encounters with the Almighty

In the Secret Place: Encounters with the Divine

In the Secret Place: Encounters in Glory

In the Secret Place: Soaking in His Glory

Leading the Way: Seniors Teaching the Next Generation

Leading the Way: Seniors Mentoring the Next Generation

Leading the Way: Seniors Lifting Up a Standard

Leading the Way: Seniors Leaving a Legacy of Righteousness

Leading the Way: Seniors Called to Serve

Seniors United to Serve

Seniors United: Taking a Stand for Christ

Seniors United and Leading the Way

Seniors United: Leaving a Legacy of Righteousness

Seniors United: Leaving a Legacy of Holiness

Seniors Called to Impact the World for Christ

Seniors On a Mission

Seasoned to Serve: Seniors Leading the Way

Seasoned to Serve: Seniors Fulfilling the Great Commission

Seasoned to Serve: Seniors Advancing the Kingdom

Seasoned to Serve: Seniors Impacting the World for Christ

Healthy, Wealthy, Wise: Seniors Taking the Kingdom for God

Healthy, Wealthy, Wise: These Are the Golden Years

Healthy, Wealthy, Wise: The Best Is Yet to Come

Healthy, Wealthy, Wise: Living Life to the Fullest

Healthy, Wealthy, Wise: Living Life God's Way

Healthy, Wealthy, Wise: Living in Perfect Balance

Healthy, Wealthy, Wise: Embracing the Golden Years

United to Stand: Living Wholly for Christ

The Power of One: Wholly Committed

Connected to Impact: One Vision, One Purpose

Single & Consecrated: Waiting on the Lord

Single & Consecrated: Giving My Heart to God

Single & Consecrated: Man in Waiting

Single & Consecrated: Woman in Waiting

Single & Consecrated: Seeking the Face of God

Single & Consecrated: Waiting in His Presence

Single & Consecrated: Living Life to the Fullest

Single & Consecrated: A Vow to Embrace Purity

Single & Consecrated: A Season of Preparation

Ignite: On Fire for God's Glory

Ignite: On Fire for Christ

Ignition: On Course for Christ

In His Presence: Developing a Devoted Lifestyle

Kingdom Connections & Divine Hook-ups

Kingdom Connections & Divine Alignment

Situated to Serve: Consecrated for the Master's Use

Situated to Serve: Consecrated for His Purpose

Living in the Secret Place: Finding My Place in Him

In the Secret Place: Waiting in the Presence of God

Woman to Woman: The Power of Covenant Relationships

Woman to Woman: Supporting the Vision

Ascend to Defend: Women Taking Their Place in the Kingdom

Divine Conceptions: Birthing the Promises of God

Girls' Night Out: Refresh and Refuel

Leading the Way: Business Women Called to Serve

Leading the Way: Business Women Called to Mentor

PUSH: Birthing Dimensional Anointings

PUSH: Birthing Dreams and Visions

PUSH: Birthing the Purposes of God

Relax, Release, Receive

Raising the Standard: When Godly Women Lead

Women Empowered for Kingdom Dominion

Women Lifting Up a Standard

Women of Destiny: Arise and Live

Women of Destiny: Your Time Is Now

Women of Destiny: Moving Beyond the Boundaries

Women of Destiny: Arising to Possess

Women of Destiny: Arising to Conquer

Women of Destiny: Arising to Overcome

Women of Destiny Arise

Women of Destiny United to Impact

Women of Destiny United to Serve

Women of Destiny United to Restore

Women of Destiny United

Women of Destiny: Advancing the Kingdom

Women of Destiny: Called to Lead

Women of Distinction: Leaving a Godly Legacy

Women of Distinction: Leaving a Legacy for the Next Generation

Women of Distinction: A Call to Action

Exceptional Women: Lifting Up a Standard

Exceptional Women: Standing Strong

Exceptional Women: Called to Impact the Next Generation

Women on the Forefront: Fortified to Fight

Women on the Forefront: Armed and Dangerous

Women on the Forefront: Called to Conquer

Sister to Sister: Building a Bridge to Destiny

Sister to Sister: Building Strong Connections

Sister to Sister: Mentoring the Next Generation

Sister to Sister: Connected as One

Sister to Sister: Breaking Down Barriers

Sister to Sister: United as One

Sister to Sister: Building Covenant Relationships

Sister to Sister: Standing United

Sister to Sister: United to Empower

Sister to Sister: Walking Together in Unity

Sisters United: I Need You to Survive

Sisters United: Lifting Up a Standard for Christ

Sisters United: Supporting the Visions of Others

Sisters United: The Power of Covenant Relationships

Sisters United for Purpose: Overcoming Together

Sisters United for Purpose: Synergistic Relationships

Sisters United for Purpose: Limitless Living

Sisters United for Purpose: Fortified Connections

Woman to Woman: Strengthening for the Journey

Woman to Woman: Building Strong Connections

Woman to Woman: Mentoring the Next Generation

Woman to Woman: Connected as One

Woman to Woman: Breaking Down Barriers

Woman to Woman: United as Sisters

Woman to Woman: Standing United

Woman to Woman: Overcoming Together

Women of Purpose Unite: Lifting Up a Standard for Christ

Women of Purpose Unite: Building Synergistic Relationships

Women of Purpose Unite: Building Covenant Relationships

Women of Purpose Unite: Fortified Connections

Women of Purpose Unite: I Need You to Survive

Women of Purpose Unite: Walking Together in Unity

Women of Purpose Unite: Standing Strong, Creating a Bond

The Great Reveal: Releasing the Queen in Me

The Great Reveal: Calling Forth the Daughters of Destiny

The Great Reveal: Women of Purpose Arise

Divine Conceptions: Birthing the Promises of God

Divine Encounters with Destiny

Divine Encounters: Stepping Behind the Veil

Divine Encounters: A Night with the King

Divine Encounters: Touched by the Manifested Presence of God

Divine Encounters: Embracing the Manifested Presence of God

Divine Encounters: Deep Calling unto Deep

Divine Encounters: Touched by the Shekinah Glory

Divine Encounters: Embracing New Realms of Glory

Divine Encounters: Moving Beyond the Veil

Divine Encounters: Moving from Glory to Glory

Divine Encounters: Understanding the Realms of the Supernatural

Divine Encounters: Accessing Supernatural Portals of God

Divine Encounters: An Intimate Affair with the King

Divine Encounters: At the Feet of Jesus

Divine Encounters: At the Throne of God

Divine Encounters: Access Granted

Divine Encounters: Embracing God's Purpose for My Life

Divine Encounters: Embracing the Purposes of God

Divine Encounters with God: Developing a Culture of Intimacy

In His Presence: Developing a Culture of Intimacy

In His Presence: Restoring the Hunger for Truth

Empowered to Possess

Empowered to Possess: Engaging the Supernatural

Empowered to Possess: Tearing Down the Barriers

Empowered to Possess: Living the Dream

Empowered to Possess: Moving Beyond the Limitations

Empowered to Possess: Living Life Without Limits

PUSH: Birthing Your Destiny

Legends in the Making

Women Birthing Destiny: A Call to Action

Women Birthing Destiny: Calling Forth God's Purpose

Women Birthing Destiny: Mother of Zion, Arise

Women Birthing Destiny: Called to Impact the Next Generation

Women Lifting Up a Standard

Women Lifting Up a Standard: Fortified to Fight

Women Lifting Up a Standard: Called to Birth God's Will

Mentoring Mothers: Establishing a Legacy of Righteousness

Mentoring Mothers: Raising Up Daughters for the Kingdom

Mentoring Mothers: Nurturing the Next Generation

Mentoring Mothers: Teaching by Example

Mentoring Mothers: Raising Up Daughters of Zion

Mentoring Mothers: Establishing a Legacy of Holiness

Mothers of Distinction: The Birthing of a Nation

Mothers of Distinction: Leaving a Legacy of Hope

Mothers of Distinction: Called to Birth God's Will

Leading the Way: Mothers Called to Serve

Leading the Way: When Godly Mothers Pray

A Call to Excellence: Young Adults Lifting Up a Standard

A Call to Excellence: Youth Lifting Up a Standard

Young Warriors: Arise and Take Your Place

Young Warriors: Possessing the Nations for Christ

Young Warriors: Reaching a Generation for Christ

United to Stand: Reaching the Family for Christ

United to Stand: Reaching a Generation for Christ

Youth Explosion: On Fire for God

Youth Explosion: Seizing the Moment for God's Purpose

Youth Explosion: Impacting the World for Christ

Licensed to Live: Giving My All for Christ

Youth Explosion: Charged Up for Christ

Youth Explosion: Lifting Up a Standard for Christ

Ignite: Stirred Up, for the Shake-Up

Ignite: Stirring Up the Flames

Ignite: Ablaze to Raise Up a Standard for Christ

Ignite: All Fired Up for Christ

Ignite: Fanning the Flames for Christ

Ignition: Driven to Serve God's Purpose

Ignition: Driven to Touch the Nations for Christ

Ignition: Driven to Serve the Community

Ignition: Driven with Passion for God

Ignition: Driven by His Presence

Refuel: On Course for Christ

Refuel: Connected to the Right Source

Refuel: Moving Forward with Christ

Refuel: Driven to Serve the Lord

Refuel: Giving God a High-Octane Praise

Refuel: Charged Up to Live for Christ

Spiritual Hysteria: Youth Crazy for Christ

Spiritual Hysteria: Young Adults Crazy for Christ

Spiritual Hysteria: Tearing Down the Walls of Religion

Spiritual Hysteria: Living in Divine Order in a Crazy World

Spiritual Hysteria: Breaking Loose for Christ

Spiritual Hysteria: Called to Change the Culture

Spiritual Hysteria: Youth Giving God a Crazy Praise

Tagged: Marked by God

Tagged: Marked for God's Purpose

Tagged: Marked to Live for Christ

Tagged: Branded for the Kingdom

Tagged: Branded with Divine Purpose

Tagged: Lifting Up a Standard for Christ

Tagged: Called to Serve Christ

Tagged: Called to Serve God's Will

Licensed to Live: Young Adults Living for Christ

Licensed to Live: Driven to Overcome

Licensed to Live: Driven to Succeed

Licensed to Live: Youth Living for Christ

EVENT JUMPSTART PLANNING WORKSHEET

Name of your event:

_____

_____

_____

Event theme:

_____

_____

_____

Event purpose:

_____

_____

_____

Event objectives:

_____

_____

_____

_____

_____

Type of event:

_____

_____

_____

Proposed speaker(s):

_____

_____

_____

Proposed venue(s):

_____

_____

_____

Branding strategy:

_____

_____

_____

_____

_____

_____

Event Jumpstart Planning Worksheet

Name of your event:

_____

_____

_____

Event theme:

_____

_____

_____

Event purpose:

_____

_____

_____

Event objectives:

_____

_____

_____

_____

_____

_____

Type of event:

_____

_____

_____

Proposed speaker(s):

_____

_____

_____

Proposed venue(s):

_____

_____

_____

Branding strategy:

_____

_____

_____

_____

_____

EVENT JUMPSTART PLANNING WORKSHEET

Name of your event:

_____

_____

_____

Event theme:

_____

_____

_____

Event purpose:

_____

_____

_____

Event objectives:

_____

_____

_____

_____

_____

_____

Type of event:

_____

_____

_____

Proposed speaker(s):

_____

_____

_____

Proposed venue(s):

_____

_____

_____

Branding strategy:

_____

_____

_____

_____

_____

Event Jumpstart Planning Worksheet

Name of your event:

_____

_____

_____

Event theme:

_____

_____

_____

Event purpose:

_____

_____

_____

Event objectives:

_____

_____

_____

_____

_____

_____

Type of event:

_____

_____

_____

Proposed speaker(s):

_____

_____

_____

Proposed venue(s):

_____

_____

_____

Branding strategy:

_____

_____

_____

_____

_____

_____

Event Jumpstart Planning Worksheet

Name of your event:

_____

_____

_____

Event theme:

_____

_____

_____

Event purpose:

_____

_____

_____

Event objectives:

_____

_____

_____

_____

_____

_____

Type of event:

_____

_____

_____

Proposed speaker(s):

_____

_____

_____

Proposed venue(s):

_____

_____

_____

Branding strategy:

_____

_____

_____

_____

_____

_____

Event Jumpstart Planning Worksheet

Name of your event:

_____

_____

_____

Event theme:

_____

_____

_____

Event purpose:

_____

_____

_____

Event objectives:

_____

_____

_____

_____

_____

Type of event:

_____

_____

_____

Proposed speaker(s):

_____

_____

_____

Proposed venue(s):

_____

_____

_____

Branding strategy:

_____

_____

_____

_____

_____

_____

For more awesome conference and event resources,
be sure to visit:
www.AwesomeEventSolutions.com

There you will find resources to help you plan a
awesome conference, meeting or special event,
plus download your
FREE Conference Planning Checklist

Tarsha L. Campbell is a dynamic Woman of Destiny! With this mandate she humbly serves as an award-winning entrepreneur, empowerment speaker, licensed minister, certified life coach and business consultant. Tarsha is the author of four popular books: Help! I've Been Called By God: Easy Steps to Preparing and Delivering a Message; 5 Qualities of a Woman of Destiny; Woman in the Mirror: A Case of Mistaken Identity; Woman in the Mirror: Ungodly Soul Ties - Break Free to Break Through. Through her speaking, coaching and consulting business, Tarsha Campbell Empowers, Tarsha's mission is to help emerging leaders identify, clarify, and take their next step. Tarsha is also the executive director of Revealed International Women's Empowerment Network, Inc., an organization dedicated to helping women unveil their God-given identity, potential, purpose and destiny. The organization's lifetime mission is to help 100,000 women unveil and fulfill their life purpose.

For over twenty years, Tarsha has planned awesome conferences and special events geared toward bringing people together to experience corporate and personal growth, life-changing empowerment and advancement. Tarsha's passions include uniting ideas and people from all walks of life to build unity and community.

Visit Tarsha's websites:

www.TarshaCampbellEmpowers.com
www.connecttoempower.com

Connect with Tarsha:

www.facebook.com/tarsha.campbell
Twitter: @CoachTarsha
Instagram: @TarshaCampbell

NOTES

www.ingramcontent.com/pod-product-compliance
Lightning Source LLC
Chambersburg PA
CBHW052207270326
41931CB00011B/2263